PASSION
TO
PREVAIL
IN
MARRIAGE

PASSION
TO
PREVAIL
IN
MARRIAGE

DR. JEANETTE D. DAVIS

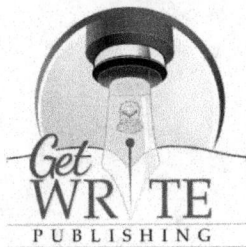

Get
WR TE
PUBLISHING

PASSION TO PREVAIL: IN MARRIAGE

Copyright © 2017 by Jeanette D. Davis

All Scripture quotations, unless otherwise indicated, are taken from the King James Bible Version.

ISBN 978-1-945456-96-1

Printed in the United States of America

Cover Design: Kevin Vain - CoLAB Creative Group

Editor: Sharlene Carter, MLS

TABLE OF CONTENTS

DEDICATIONS

This book is first and foremost dedicated to my Lord and Savior Jesus Christ who by his grace blessed our marriage and blessed me with the knowledge to publish this book. I pray the ministry of this book be pleasing in HIS sight.

To my husband Dr. Phillip Davis. Without you this book would not be possible. It is because of the Love we have built, share and continue to build that thrust my inspiration. I love you so much and thank you for being an awesome man of God and a wonderful husband. Thank you for your contribution of wisdom in writing this book.

To my children Shanae Denise and Jamar Rashad, (Proverbs 18:22 The man who finds a wife finds a treasure, and he receives favor from the Lord (NLT). I pray this scripture be manifested in both of your lives. I love you and grandson Elijah.

To my parents Walter and Fannie M. Harkless and brother Derrick Harkless thank you so very much for your continued love and support and always being there. You are the best and I love you.

To My Brother and Sister in Law/Love, Elder Gary and Deborah Davis thank you for your love and support and being there with your encouragement and belief in our marriage ministry over the years. Blessings to you and your family.

To Elder Booker T. and Mary Presley our mentors, our friends and our family thank you for being a blessing in our marriage. Your love, friendship and support for over the past 20 plus years is invaluable and unmeasurable.

To Elder Edward and Sharlene Carter, words cannot express my thanks to you both for your friendship, support, wisdom and labor of love during this process. I am forever grateful.

To the anointed Pastors of past and present, Teachers and Mentors that we have had the privilege to serve and follow you as you follow Christ thank you for entrusting us to stand in marriage ministry during our time with you.

To Dr. Robert F. Dowell, Pastor New Life Fellowship Church who taught much wisdom and knowledge to move forward in the ministry of marriage. We both sincerely thank you for launching us out and pulling what God had imparted in us to the forefront. Great blessings to you, First Lady Alicia Dowell, your family and the Ministry.

To Alvin and Ruth Brumfield, thank you for touching both of our lives with your love.

To the reader, blessings to each one of you having a love, dedication, strength and willingness to strive in taking your marriage to a greater level. I celebrate the deep love, compassion and desire you have for your spouse and I applaud you for reading and applying this book into your life.

FOREWORD

Passion to Prevail: In Marriage written by Dr. Jeanette Davis needs to be in the library of every married couple.

Marriage is an instrumental part of God's plan for humanity.

If couples are going to be a success in this great union that was created, ordained and instituted by God, they will need the proper tools, teaching, and training.

This book provides couples with incredible information, revelation, and inspiration that they need to be victorious in their marriage.

Throughout this book, Dr. Davis gives practical and powerful principles that if implemented will infuse husbands and wives with a passion to prevail in their marriage.

In chapter six Dr. Davis shares words of wisdom on how a wife can celebrate her husband.

I have witnessed Dr. Davis live these principles for over 19 years.

She has not only penned an awesome book, but she has also lived and walked out the teachings in it.

It has also been a distinct honor and pleasure for me to witness her husband Dr. Phillip Davis exhibit what it means to love your wife as Christ loves the church.

Just as Dr. Phillip inspired the writings of chapters 4, 5 and 6, he has likewise inspired many husbands to use the proper keys to become the godly spouse God has called them to be.

Together, as a husband and wife team, Drs. Phillip and Jeanette are models and mentors that are called by God to help couples overcome challenges and experience the very best in their marriages.

As you read this book, prepare to receive a fresh anointing that will empower you with a *Passion To Prevail: In Marriage*.

Dr. Robert F. Dowell
Senior Pastor,
New Life Fellowship
Lawton, Oklahoma

INTRODUCTION

Marriage is not for the faint at heart but for those who have a passion to prevail, to triumph and to overcome every obstacle and challenge in marriage through change, determination and perseverance.

Passion to Prevail: In Marriage speaks to the heart of marriage addressing the hidden thoughts, acts and feelings.

Passion to Prevail: In Marriage will equip you with necessary tools in making marriage better from communicating the vision and direction for your marriage to wisdom in celebrating your spouse.

After reading this book and allowing yourself to be free and to be real in your marriage, you will seek to truly desire real love, not perfect love.

Rather this is for you, for your ministry or a couple's book club this tool of ministry will propel you to endure with passion, fire and stamina to stay married.

Stirring up your passion so you can prevail.

GEAR UP!

CLIMB THE MOUTAIN OF MARRIAGE AND PREVAIL

G – Give what you expect to receive.
E – Endurance to stay in the race.
A – Accept each other's differences.
R – Reconcile past issues.

Chapter One

Keeping Marriage Real

Marriage is not for the faint at heart but for those who have a passion for prevailing, to triumph and to overcome. It's not enough to be an adult of age, but you must be mature to endure.
You need passion, fire and stamina to stay married.

The Bible tells us *that the race is not given to the swift nor the strong but to the one that can endure.* Ecclesiastes 9:11.

The same thing applies to marriage. There must be a drive that causes you to stand in your for better or for worse. Marriage is not a fairy tale it's a real life thing. Marriage is not a Lifetime movie with a brief short story that lasts for two hours. Nor is it an illusion of ones' entire life

Anything can be perfect, excellent and easy for two hours but when you're talking two years, 20 years and so on the challenges will come. Movie props are used to set the stage, the scenery and to make the scene seem realistic for those who watch the film.

Have you ever notice that just at the right look you can see the Eiffel Tower in the background as if the actors are in Paris? They speak the right words as written in the script and at the right moment, the perfect music starts to play. The couple falls into each other's arms then the music elevates, and then it comes; the perfect kiss. Next, in the background, the sun starts to go down.

The woman looks beautiful, and the man looks beyond handsome. Then all of a sudden, the director yells, "Cut!" Now it's time to get ready for the next scene, which is the perfect outside wedding, but take note. You have this beautiful outside wedding, and you never see a bug, fly, gnat or anything that would make sense moving about. The cake never leans to one side as mine did at an indoor wedding reception; why, because it's a movie scene. The wedding does not take place outside nor in Paris. A computer generates the Parisian scene, the sunlight is staged by lights to betray a sunset, and the outdoor wedding is in a prop room on the inside of a studio.

None of it is real, not even the people. They are actors pretending to be somebody else.

All, of this, is a wedding scene showing how a production company produces a movie or show, but the sad part is too many couples are trying to take this same approach in real marriages.

Are you setting the stage to make your marriage look real? *In reality, your marriage may not be at all what other's see nor may it be what you the couple claim it to be.*

Pretense comes in when passion goes out.

Pretense comes in because no one wants to be real with themselves, each other or with God. We have pretended so much in our marriages that we don't even know what's real and what's not. I am often leery of people who over publicize how much they love each other to where it seems unreal.

Suspicious of couples who puff their spouses up and sell them to others all the time. Such an act can seem a little doubting, and it seems as if there are some insecurities or issues that they have to cover up.

It is not the things that are right that we are walking in that are destroying the marriage or cause the marriage not to prevail. It is the things that are wrong and the things that we don't acknowledge, address, work on or change that is destroying the marriage and cause a resulting in lost passion.

We can walk around pretending that everything is alright and not allow or receive help, advice or ministry from anyone. We can only pretend for so long trying to escape the reality of the issues at hand acting as if things do not exist. We pretend that we are so much in love in public but behind closed doors, there is no love.

Because we are tired of where we are and who we are with we can open the door for adultery to slip in.

Now, don't get me wrong it is a beautiful thing to build up your spouse, and you need to build up your spouse.

We should cover our spouses and not expose their short comings, weakness or faults. If we keep pretending and imagining what it's like to be with someone else if not careful we will eventually try to make that become a reality. When watching love scenes and movies with perfect props and settings, be careful. If not careful; we can start comparing our marriage and become sadden because it does not look like what appears in the movie or television screen.

In fact, on the flip side, *some that are walking in great marriages can destroy their marriage because they are wanting and desiring something that is not real.* You may have a good wife or a good husband, but you are focusing on all the things you feel are wrong and have forgotten about all the things they do and have done right.

You see Sally or Joe *(these are just examples)* do one thing right that you think is great and now you are comparing your spouse to them. *You can destroy your marriage quickly by comparing your spouse to someone else.* You are now trying to make your spouse be like Sally or Joe. Women, be careful not to have preconceived ideas about how the man should give you the world and put pressure on your husband to make things happen. Men, you can also put the same pressure on yourselves in following the actions of another person.

Don't set goals to give and receive the world but to give and receive what you can.

Pressure points occur when too much responsibility is placed on one person to carry the weight and the support of the family and give beyond one's limitations. Just like a pressure cooker somehow the steam must be released.

The small situation that happens with the children or when talking about something insignificant can cause pressure to build up and seep out. If it doesn't seep out in tiny spouts, the pressure will eventually build up, and an explosion will take place. Wives support your husbands and husbands support your wives' so that pressure points don't build up. Refrain from focusing on what you don't have and acknowledge what you do have.

Appreciate your spouse for who they are and not what you want them to be. *The truth is if your spouse were to tell you how they really feel at times, you are not all he/she want you to be either, but they love you anyway.* *We're talking about the passion* for prevailing in your marriage, right here.

To keep or restore the passion, there must be a change. The change comes from within you and not just within your spouse.

You have to live out the duration of the commitment. Live it out through changes and through up and downs. Change is lived out through the highs and the lows and through the good, the bad and the ugly.

To prevail in marriage learning how to handle one's insecurities is needed.

When we are not fulfilled spiritual, emotionally or vocationally, we can look for the lack of what we need in the other spouse. It is surprising how many marriages are experiencing this very thing from time to time. Imagine if you will that it is possible that in your pure and holy marriage that at some point you could experience un-fulfillment.

Your spouse does not complete you!

Too many times we are looking for our spouses to complete us by filling a void that they cannot fill. Not feeling that your husband or wife doesn't compliment you enough and having a desire to be applauded will open the door for adultery.

Encourage yourself, praise yourself.

Look in the mirror and tell yourself how good you look. Look in the mirror and speak what is written in the Word of God about who you are.

You need to fill the void with passion, grace, and destiny that the Lord destined you to be and what you are to do.

This is discussed in chapter two, *Passion to Prevail: Victory in Life*. The empty space and void can arise when and if you or your spouse are lacking the passion for prevailing in your life as individuals.

How do we avoid the empty space in marriage? You avoid the empty space by watching and safeguarding your words.

Proverbs 10:11 states; The mouth of a righteous man is a well of life, but violence covereth the mouth of the wicked.

Your words should be a fountain of life that rolls off your tongue into and over your spouse like a cold drink of water on a hot summer day in the desert. So, speak soothing and sweet saturating words with love and comfort when you talk. Your words should speak life. Read *Proverbs 18:21.*

Life and death is in the power of the tongue so your words should express affirmation to your spouse. Your words should show affection, acceptance and they should be words of praise, and your words should never be harsh.

Proverbs 15:1 A soft answer turneth away wrath: but grievous words stir up anger. New Living Translation reads, A gentle answer deflects anger, but harsh words make tempers flare.

A harsh word can just straight set it off!

It doesn't matter how long you have been married, saved, what title you hold, what business you own, how holy you are, how much experience and education you may have or how much you love the Lord.

The wrong word at the right time could change an atmosphere.

Ephesians 4:26- We are human and still can get angry that is why the word says to be angry and sin not.

Evaluate the situation before speaking.

Something may have been said out of turn at that moment. But when you evaluate the situation, you realize it was not just about that moment.

When you look at the entire picture it's not about that moment, but about the weapon that was trying to form for a time greater than that moment. You or your spouse may have been preparing for an interview, ministry assignment, a test or preparing for an important mission and a trap was being set to throw you or your spouse off focus. We must guard our words. Not just what is said, but how words are spoken and know that not every word require a response. Always evaluate the situation past that moment.

Avoid empty space by sharing quality time

Genesis 2:18- And the LORD God said, It is not good that the man should be alone; I will make him an help meet for him.

<u>No one should be married and lonely or alone</u>.

You don't want to open the door for your spouse to seek companionship somewhere else. Women spend time with your man.

The Word says it's not good that man should be alone which is why we were created. You were formed from the dust of the earth for your spouse. If we are not careful, we can be saved, be focused and passionate in being created to worship the Lord and neglect the time for passion in the marriage. There is a time for worship and a time for your marital relationship.

Worship means: love, reverence, respect, adore, devotion.

There is a time when you need to render love, admiration, respect, adoration, devotion to your spouse. If you want to be treated like a queen or king, then you need to see him or her as a king or queen giving him or her love and respect.

Likewise, husbands, you are to love your wife as Christ loves the church. Those that you love you spend time with. No one should be giving your wife more time and attention than you. *No one should be giving your spouse more comments and compliments than you. She is your queen, she is your favor.*

The Word of God tells us in Proverbs 18:22 he that findeth a wife finds a good thing and obtain favor with the Lord.

Cover your favor! Cover with your love, prayer, time and attention.

Why do you think you see people who have been married for 10, 15, 20, 30, and 40 years getting a divorce? Its passion left in the marriage. You look on the outside and say they got it going on, they have beautiful children, a nice car, nice home, nice clothes what more could they possibly want?

They want love, soft words, quality time and some companionship. I have heard and hear older couples saying all the time, "we spend quality time together quite often."
So, I ask them the question; when was the last time you've been on a date?

Frequently I receive no answer, and I hear the sound of crickets rubbing their hind legs together in the still of the night.

Straight silence. So now I ask you, when is the last time you and your spouse went on a real date? For those of you who are reading and you were able to answer with a smile and high five your spouse because the dating life with each other is truly grand. I say "hats off to you!" I had many men respond to the dating question say, "I take my wife out, and we date all the time." She cooked dinner, and we watched the game together while we ate.

That's nice, but was it set up as a date? If I ask some couples, "when was the last time you all had a romantic evening", they may respond we date and we eat out all the time.

If it was just the purpose of getting a meal because you were hungry and nothing was cooked at home or going through the drive thru it doesn't count. It doesn't count as a date if one of you does not see it as one.

So, you're eating out and making a drive thru run more than likely was not a date. Now if you have purposed to date and you both acknowledge it as being a date then it's a date. If you are going through the drive thru or sitting at the drive-in restaurant to eat for your date night, it's a date enjoy it.

When is the last time you had one of those date nights that took a lot of heart and passion and planning? A date that you had to put a lot of thought into. I'm talking candle light, soft music, a meal, or an evening out of town at a hotel get a way. I'm talking about one of those good ole' dates where you take your wife or husband out and treat him or her like you did when you were on your quest to conquer and gain their love.

Whew! You want to talk about stirring up the passion for prevailing in your marriage, set up one of those passionate dates for your husband or for your wife thinking only of all the things that you love about them and the things you enjoy in them. Believe me, when I say that will spark a passion for sure.

I feel passion stirring in me right now, and I'm just writing about it. In marriage, we must *fight to keep the Fire Flaming.*

"Father I pray that there will be a stirring of fire and passion in marriages that their love and marriage will prevail over every situation, circumstance and over every trial and that marriages will soar to the next level in Jesus Name. Amen."

Okay, now let's get back to the empty space.

Avoid empty space by giving emotional support and intimacy

Having time to just cuddle, hold each other, kiss and expressing love that doesn't have to lead to anything else is emotional and intimate time together.

A hug, a touch, and prayer over and with your spouse are all emotional support. Times of just listening, sharing things concerning each other's lives such as ministry, career or business. Ministry support from the spouse is needed. Be sure to keep your titles out of your bedroom and personal time.

If not careful we can get so focused on our business, titles and ministry positions that we forget to just be a wife or a husband. Okay, so I'm going back to the date thing. Seriously, set a date night or weekend getaway for just the two of you. This is essential for those of you in ministry, Pastors, Elders, Ministers, etc., a getaway is a must.

For those of you who may minister to couples, you need to have couples getaway time for yourself. Planning a marriage retreat and speaking at is not a date it is still ministry work. Be sure to attend Marriage Retreats or events outside of your own local church or organization. Attend, be a part and receive information and wisdom to apply to your own marriage. When is the last time you forgot about everything? The bills, finances, family members, children, people on the job and just focused on the two of you. Being together and enjoying each other's company so much that even in a crowded atmosphere you feel as if you are the only two in the room. All your focus is on your spouse, and all your husband/wife focus is on you.

Make a promise to each other that when you are on a date, those subjects are off limits. They can interrupt and change the atmosphere of the date. Sometimes you need to pull out that old song that reminds you of when you first met or when you first fell in love with one another. Pull out your wedding song and listen to it together it can pull you in and enhance your relationship with your spouse at the appropriate time with just the two of you. Talk about the good times and reminisce about the things that made you both laugh. *Live and fall in love with each other all over again. Keep your marriage from being staged by being real and staying real with God. Stir up the passion so that you can prevail you have many more years to go.*

Psalm 91:16-With long life, the Lord shall satisfy you.

The two of you have been through and seen a lot over the years, and you have also come far over the years and didn't give up.

What do you think it was that kept you from giving up? I can tell you. What kept you from giving up was passion. Passion requires having the heart for something.

That is why *it is more important for couples to have moments of intense discussions at times that mean there is a passion.*

When there is no passion, and the sparks are fading, then there are no longer moments of intense discussion but silence.

Once the talking stops the love disappears. This often comes from undealt with marital issues between couples.

Anything from your past not dealt with in your future will become out of control.

Just like a snowball effect. If you take a snowball and just continue to roll it in the snow, it becomes larger. Imagine past issues, ways, attitude, etc. being a snowball rolling in the snow and each year those unresolved issues, ways, and attitude are not dealt with they become massive.

So much so that you can no longer roll it. It now rolls over you.

Any areas in your marriage that need to be addressed, please attend to them before they address you and *Never leave your bed.*

When you leave your bed, you leave room for thoughts, hurt and loneliness to affect you both. We hear it often that the enemy is after marriages.

It is written in the word of God that the enemy walks about as a roaring lion seeking whom he may devour. (1 Peter 5:8)

Do you Remember the game mother may I? The person will say, mother, may I take two steps and you would say; "yes you may!" And if you didn't want them to because they asked the wrong thing you would answer; "no you may not!" The same things with marriages; we have the choice to say yes and take two steps, or we have the option to say "no you may not," and just hold up right there! For the enemy to destroy your marriage, you have to give him two steps forward or give him something to work with. The same thing with the Lord, we must give the Lord something to work with in our marriages. You are either going to let the enemy work, the Lord work or try to figure it out yourself and let your flesh work. And I can tell you now that will not work.

No weapon formed against us shall be able to prosper. (Isiah 54:17)

However, we must be sure we are not forming our own weapons within ourselves or fighting against the weapons that you create yourself in your marriage. If you have been married for a long time, you know that marriage is still a work in progress that is never complete. It takes continued effort and time to nurture a marriage.

Do whatever it takes to keep the passion and to stir up the passion in your marriage.

There is a call for you to prevail and to succeed in your covenant.

Let this be the day that you make the declaration even the more to keep passion so that you can prevail in your marriage.

No one has it all together

Let me take a moment and talk to those who feel the need to look and act like they got it all together, but deep down inside you are dying and feel too ashamed or afraid to get help. Let me share this example with you.

This is just an example, not a diagnosis.

Many times terminal diseases sneak up in a person's life because they did not take proper care of their bodies. There were no outward symptoms. They look good, dress well and everything appears to be well on the outside so they did not go to the doctor and get proper checkups as they should have.

They do not make their physicals and yearly exams as they should. They do not make an appointment as soon as their symptoms start.

So by the time they go to the doctor after letting the pain get so bad, it is too late, and there is nothing else to do to treat their illness. All that can be done at this point is let it run its course and comfort the patient. The same thing can happen within marriages.

The couple looks good on the outside, but if appointments for marriage maintenance are missed; the marriage dies in the home.

This is why it is so important to continue to nurture your marriage no matter how long you have been married. Start reaching out to a life line. Get someone in your life that can pour into you, help you and encourage you in your marriage.

Sometimes just having someone there to mediate a conversation between you and your spouse is all that is needed to help two people understand, see and hear what the other is trying to express. Many times we can talk, but if I only listen to what I am saying and my spouse only listens to what they are saying we can't understand each other.
Fellowship and pull on other married couples when the opportunity presents itself.

Don't be concerned with what other people think about you; all you need to be concerned with is what God thinks, and He is concerned about the things that affect you.

Be real with each other, be real with yourself, be real with God and watch your marriage flourish even higher.

Ecclesiastes 4:9-12, New Living Translation
9 Two people are better off than one, for they can help each other succeed. 10 If one person falls, the other can reach out and help.

But someone who falls alone is in real trouble. 11 Likewise, two people lying close together can keep each other warm. But how can one be warm alone? 12 A person standing alone can be attacked and defeated, but two can stand back-to-back and conquer.

Do whatever it takes for your marriage to endure to the end so you both can be in joy and have happiness.

Fall in love with the spouse that you married all over again. As you continue to make your request known unto God and you both submit to one another change will come.

Pray this prayer: *Father in the Name of Jesus, draw us closer to one another. Stir up a passion for prevailing in our marriage over every circumstance and situation. What you have joined together let no man not even ourselves separate in Jesus Name. Amen.*

Now move forward and prevail.

Chapter Notes

Chapter Two

Desire Real Love Not Perfect Love

Real love can last through almost anything because there is a foundation to hold on to.

What we see as Perfect love is pretense and imaginary and contains no substance it's merely based on emotion and circumstances.

The pretense is a hollow shell where the bottom can drop out at any time when too much weight is applied. To keep the passion, you must change and allow your spouse to change.

Prevail in your marriage through seasons of unhappiness, Stay faithful to your vows.

What does happy mean?

Delighted or pleased. Characterized by or indicative of pleasure of joy.

Ephesians 5:21 - Submitting yourselves one to another in the fear of God.

Many times we want to leave our spouses because our spouse won't change. Often times we are looking for our spouse to fulfill our every need.

Why do you think so many marriages fail right in the house of God and we have all the Word and all the Jesus that we could desire? On the flip side, why do you think so many marriages fail in Hollywood, with the money and all the luxury that they could desire?

Could it be because in the church they are looking for that spouse to do and to be in their life what only God can do and be? The people in Hollywood and with all their riches can't seem to figure out both why they can't seem to find the right spouse and can't manage to find the right formula to make a marriage work.

With all the Word that the people in the House of God receive and all the Word that they preach, but yet sometimes it is still a struggle, and they can't seem to find the formula to build a happy marriage either.

Could it be because those who don't know God are looking for their spouse to be their God? Could it be that those in the House of God are not allowing God to be the focal point in their marriage?

When we are looking for your spouse to fulfill your every need and when they don't how many times the answer to that is the two magic words. I'm gone!

Many times, heads bump in marriage because one spouse is looking for the other spouse to change, but the person looking for change doesn't want to change themselves.

You can manage to see and point out all of your husband or wife faults but forget about your own. Often times we make the grand decision to leave because our spouse is not willing to change. I don't recall seeing that as a part of the marriage vows. I remember these words: will you (insert name) take (*insert name*) to be your husband/wife? Will you commit yourself to his/her happiness and his/her self-fulfillment as a person, and to his/her usefulness in God's Kingdom?

Will you promise to love, honor, trust and serve him/her in sickness and in health, in adversity and prosperity, and to be true and loyal to him/her so long as you both shall live?

I don't see anywhere where it says if they don't change you are free to leave. Now I am not trying to dictate your life's decision.

I am just merely sharing food for thought.

The marriage vows are not something we can fancy up. Let them be what they are and say what they need to say so we can do what we need to do in our marriages. From time to time it's good to remind ourselves of what our marriage vows were.

We should love the person that we married, not just love them when we feel they are who we want them to be.

Many times wanting to leave a marriage doesn't really have anything to do with our spouses needing to change.
Sometimes, we want to leave because we are not willing to change the hidden issues and that is why we are so unhappy.

It's not usually adultery, physical abuse or even mental abuse it's frequently a problem in our own heart or in the heart of our spouse that hasn't been dealt with.

It is typically the unresolved insecurities, past hurts, disappointments, unforgiveness, and brokenness that you had before your wedding day. Issues that you dressed up, hid and tucked away from on lookers and soon to be spouse. As you walked down the aisle or waited at the altar, you carried them, and they stood beside you.

Picture it big smiles on your faces, him in his nice tuxedo and you shining brightly in your beautiful dress or whatever you wore on your wedding day and wherever the location was. The outward appearance of the perfect couple so very much in love was displayed.

While on the inside there may have remained past or recent hurts, pains or secrets that all stood there with you.

When the judge, minister or whoever married you said: "do you take?"

You said yes, "I do!" At that moment when you said I do you did. What exactly did you do? You said yes, you accepted and joined your inner person and your spouse's inner person together for a life time union.

Take my story for example though this was in 1989; I walked down the aisle as a woman who was functioning, seemed to be strong but broken on the inside.

Now my aisle was the aisle at the court house, and the altar was in front of the judge's desk in his office. So on our 15 year anniversary, we celebrated with a wedding and great honeymoon. *That was just a little side note*. Back to my original wedding day.

On that day I showed much security in myself. I was living on my own, taking care of myself and a little baby girl to the best of my ability. I had no money, no car and sometimes

I had no lights. Did things get better? Sure they did, but it took some time.

This was a result of choices, actions and decisions made during that season of my life.

Meanwhile, the time of year was the deciding factor in me making the selection of what bills would be paid. If the season was winter, we could go without the lights using candles because we needed the gas for heat and cooking as my stove was gas, and so was my furnace.

So, it was a good time of the year for the gas company. If it was summer, we could do without the gas and keep the electric because we needed the electricity for the air conditioner and it was warm enough to do without the gas. I needed the electrical power to maintain the refrigerator and to keep food cold.

You get the picture? Although this season in my life didn't last long, the fact is that it happened and I lived through it. For a season I had no vehicle, so I had to get a ride here and there although my dad later was able to bless me with a nice car.

What kept me and caused me to push through this season of my life was the passion that I had to survive in my heart.

I had the appearance of strength on the outside, and I honestly thought I was, but unaware I was still struggling on the inside from life's disappointments, upsets, hurts, changes and responsibilities that I could never imagine would be my world at that time of life. Now back to the altar on the wedding day.

The judge was waiting for me to respond to his question; will you take this man?

Yes, I take this man who also stood there looking robust and secure a man who I saw as my knight in shining armor having it all together. I later found out he also stood beside me with hidden issues and also was overcoming life's changes, responsibilities and challenges. As we both stood there saying I do; we later discovered we really didn't know who we were saying I do too.

We committed to the outer shell that was visible while the inner shell was covered. Like I said this was in 1989.

Through, in and by the grace of God we have succeeded to grow and stay together all these years because we were willing to be healed, change, learn from others and most importantly put the Lord first in our lives and in our marriage.

We had a passion for prevailing in our marriage no matter what. I'm sharing all of that to say this.

Everyone started in marriage somewhere and as the years go by you grow up, and you change, but the key in that is to allow your husband or your wife to do the same, to grow up and to change.

After we get to a place and point in life to where we feel we have reached the place called there we may not be as sensitive.

We have matured and reached a certain level in the Lord, and we believe the other spouse has not we tend to get frustrated with them not being where they need to be or where we feel they need to be.

You then ask yourself how long I must keep on putting up with all of your immaturity.

Surely you should have gotten over all of that; grown up and changed!

It's been years, surely you should be over what you went through in your past by now.

That could be true, but give your spouse the love, time and ministry needed to get to that place of growth and healing.

Now if you are the spouse who is still dealing with issues and have not grown past their past. It's time for you to move forward. Stop holding on and let go.

May I suggest that you read the chapter, Facing your Pain and Releasing the Peace in the book *Passion To Prevail: Victory In Life.*

You will find a passion for prevailing in your marriage and so will your spouse.

In marriage, it's not always about where or how you started, but it's about where you are headed.

The only way to go anywhere is to get direction, move forward and move together.

Many times we are unhappy because we have allowed our spouse's emotions to become our emotions.

Be concerned, but not consumed.

If they are up you are up, if they are sad you are sad, if they get mad, you get mad. Why? That makes the situation worse than what it has to be. Doing that is like living life on a roller coaster.

It's up to you to keep stability in your emotions so that you can bring stability to the marriage.

Don't make your spouse be the air that you breathe leave that for God to be. Don't let your life be centered on your husband or wife.

Depending on your mate too much can cause them to feel overwhelmed, smothered and weighted down. Especially if they feel they have to juggle to live up to your expectations of them.

Pull up from the end of your rope and move past your feelings.

Now, let me talk to the couple or the spouse who feels like they are at the end of their rope reading this.

While in the process of wanting and waiting for things to change you may need to be willing to change.

Maybe change your attitude, how you view things and situations.

Be prepared that *until you see a change, you will be the change you want to see while you wait.*

Philippians 4:8- Finally, brethren, whatsoever things are true, whatsoever things are honest, whatsoever things are just, whatsoever things are pure, whatsoever things are lovely, whatsoever things are of good report; if there be any virtue, and if there be any praise, think on these things.

If we change our thoughts about our marriage and our spouse although things may not have changed the situation can change because your focus has changed.

There have been times some have wanted to end a marriage because of feeling like they don't love their spouse anymore. Feelings?

Lust is a feeling, but Love is a choice.

It doesn't take much to operate out of lust, but it takes work, commitment and a decision to operate out of love.

I'm sure Jesus felt emotional like coming down from the cross, but because of His choice to love us before we loved Him Jesus stayed on the cross.

We don't live, operate and do what we want and say what we want because of our feelings.

Sometimes you are at the end of your rope but never climb the rope due to the risk of rope burn. Now, this is where the choice to prevail has to come in.

In overcoming and triumphing in anything, there is going to be work.

We all want the longevity of being married, but don't want to work at it to get there. To climb any mountain, you must use the rope, and you cannot stop climbing in the middle of the mountain because it's too hard.

Can you imagine climbing a mountain, and in the midst of it look down and realize that is too high up and when you look up you feel you are too far down, but the reality of it is you are right in the middle?

It will take the same amount of work to get back down as it will take to continue up after all both ways are the same distance and will still require you to work and climb.

There is no gain in going back down the mountain, and all the work you did to get to that point is lost, however, if you stick with it and keep climbing you will reach the peak of the mountain and stand on the mountain top.

Rest right there for just a few seconds and catch your second wind and start climbing again.

Learn how to equip yourself with the right gear and tackle that mountain after you have geared up.

What type of Gear do we need to climb this mountain of marriage?

G – Give what you expect to receive in
   Marriage.
E – Endurance to stay in the race.
A – Accept each other's differences and be
   Willing to learn each other.
R– Reconcile all past issues.

Give, Endure, Accept, Reconcile

It is true that you are going to get rope burns, kicks and bruises and scrapes climbing this mountain called marriage, but keep going and ask God for strength to endure.

Remember, the Joy of the Lord is your strength. Joy up in Him and walk in His strength.

Desire: Longing, Craving

The desire for your spouse should cause your taste buds to salivate and crave for more with every bite of their love.

Dr. JDD

Chapter Three

How to Stay Focused on the Needs of Your Wife

For the Husband. *Proverbs 18:22 reads Whosoever findeth a wife findeth a good thing, and obtaineth favour of the LORD.*
New Living Translation reads; The man who finds a wife finds a treasure, and he receives favor from the Lord.

Why does it matter that you focus on your wife's needs you may ask?

It's important because she is your favor. She is your treasure, and you receive favor in your life because of her.

To stay focused on your wives needs, you first need to know what they are.

Some of your wife's needs may change as she changes and as situations in her life change, but her need for you to focus on her never changes.

Not all women are the same just because they are women, not all of their needs are the same. They have some basics needs, but they are different in character.

In 1 Corinthians 7:3 it says; Let the husband render unto the wife due benevolence: and likewise also the wife unto the husband.

A man should fulfill his duty as a husband, and a woman should fulfill her duty as a wife, and each should satisfy the other's needs.

Now let's focus on the needs of your wife.

Focus on Her Emotional Needs

<u>Women need to have their husbands express UNCONDITIONAL LOVE to them</u>.
Men, you make your marriage's work when you satisfy your wife's need to feel that unconditional love from you.

It is your duty and your responsibility to make her feel loved. Know that when that woman feels loved it doesn't matter what happens, she will stay right there.

She will stay right there when financial difficulties come, friends go, job loss. She will be there because she is loved.

You can lose everything, live in a one room shack and drive an old beat up car, but if that woman knows that she is loved she will be right there with you smiling.

Women are relational, and they have relational needs. They love relationship, and they love having a relationship with you. Ask yourself this question.

Why do you think that women can see each other and don't even know each other, but yet hold a long conversation?

Or they can see an old friend hold a conversation like they just seen each other yesterday and talk for hours.

It's because part of their emotional need is the need for relationships.

Why do you think women can talk to each other every day and still have something to say tomorrow?

It's because they have a level of attachment and relationship because women are relational beings. This is why it is so easy for women to walk in relationship with the Lord.

It is easy for women to surrender to a relationship, but even still they need and desire to have a spiritual relationship with you too.

Husband, your wife, wants to pray with you, to worship with you and to praise God with you!

Focus on Her Spiritual Needs

Your wife wants and needs to talk about the Word with you just like they do another sister or friend. Who better to discuss the Word with than the priest of her home?

When you focus on your wife's relational needs, she will concentrate on every need that you have without you even asking.

Stay focused on her needs by knowing how she needs for you to talk to her

Colossians 3:19; Husbands, love your wives, and be not bitter against them. The New Living Translation Colossians 3:19 reads "Husbands give your wife much love and never treat her harshly."

Your wife needs for you to talk to her in a straightforward and caring way regardless of what the situation is. If your wife expresses to you that she does or is not liking the way that you are talking to her or that she wishes or ask you to speak to her differently you should not respond to her " *that is just the way I am!"* She has just expressed a need to you; please, try not to ignore it. She knows that you are a man of strength and stature those are things she loves and adores about you, but the need for her to see great strength in you through love and self-control is essential.

If you reply to her; "I don't need to respond to you or talk to you the way you want me to." Answer this; why don't you or why not?

If you are to please your wife and focus on her needs, then you should adjust the way that you speak to her if she asks you to because if you don't talk to her the way she wants and desires to be spoken to then who will?

There is another question I ask that you ponder.

If that is just how you are, explain why is it that you can have control when speaking to others, but not when it comes to talking to your wife?

I know the Lord says to love your neighbor but in *Ephesians 5:33 the Bible tells you to love your wife as Christ loved the church.*

This is just a little food for thought.

Focus on your wife needs by not allowing pride to keep you from changing

Mistakes that happened in past relationships or what you saw your father do when you were growing up or just being set in your ways can keep you from changing if you don't focus on changing.

Change is growth and growth is change.

Having a successful marriage is not based on or off of what worked for your parents or other unions.

A successful marriage requires the husband and wife doing whatever it takes to make it work for them.

A successful marriage is finding what works through trial and error.

It's successful by taking the time and discovering what works for you through wisdom that is caught, embraced and applied.

Focus on your wife's needs by learning her and what pleases her

*These Action Examples were inspired by
5 Love Languages, Gary Chapman*

1.   Words of Validation and Confirmation

Tell her how good she looks and how she still turns you on.

Tell her how she's still as beautiful to you now as she was then. Tell her you love her and what you like and love about her.

If she asks for you to tell her what you love about her or if she asks you do you love her, please try not to respond by saying things like, "if I didn't love you then I would not be married to you."

Asking questions like why do I need to tell you I love you or what I love about you? Are you having feelings of insecurity?

That is not an expression of affirmation that is an insult.

She just expressed her need to hear from you about how you feel about her, and you basically gave her a slap in the face.

Please, no face slapping. Let your wife know that she is important to you.

Let her know how great of a mother she is to the children and not just on Mother's Day.

Share with her what you see in her and what she means to you. After all, this is the woman that you have chosen to spend the rest of your life with so, why not tell her and reaffirm to her what she means to you.

2.   Spend Time with Her

Quantity time does not mean quality time

Long years of marriage do not represent quality years of marriage. This is why so many marriages don't make it.

They had time but no quality. I have witnessed husbands and wives live together, sleep together, eat together, spend money together, vacation together, socializes together, raise children together, worship together, but in all of that, they never had quality time. They just had the time of movement and activities.

They vacationed with the kids went to bed tired, so they never talked. They ate their meals and as soon as they were finished left the table they did not stay for the quality time and conversation. Spouses talked more with friends than with each other.

Everything was centered on and around their children and not each other.

If it is truly quality time, then it should be focused time on her.

Listen to her conversation without listening with the anticipation for her to hurry up and get the conversation over.

Not listing and waiting for her just to get to the point, state the facts and be done.

If it is quality time, then you have nowhere to go, so that means you have time to listen. She needs that quality time with you.

Watching a movie together, listening to music together or whatever you all do for the quality time she needs.

Spending time with your wife is valuable when you have enjoyed the time you had together.

3.   Give your wife Gifts from Time to Time

If her needs are gifts, take a few dollars from time to time not on any particular occasion and get her something.

Stop wondering why when you tell her that you love her and say all that mushy stuff she just looks at you and says okay, that is not her language of love.

Purchase a gift man!

Not what you want her to have but what she would like to have.

It doesn't have to be something big or extravagant but just something to say; I LOVE YOU! A little something, something to say I am thinking about you.

4.   Show your Wife Love with your Actions

If it's chores; washing the car, walking the dog or whatever you do for her because she asked you or whatever you do to show how much you love her, do it with love. If you do it with murmuring and complaining it is not love, and an act of service to her, it is now just an act. Your wife should never see you more excited and enthusiastic to help and do something for someone else than you are to do something for her. *Outside of God, she is the most esteemed person and the most important relationship in your life even before your children.*

5. Give your Wife Warmth, Love, and Kindness

Focus on your wives needs by showing her physical affection that does not end with making love. I know the husband is now asking; "if nothing isn't going down why I am doing all of this touching and holding then?"

Because she needs it and now whatever happens after that touching and holding let it happen but if nothing happens it's still okay.

Sometimes she just wants to be held and touched with no intent involved but just know if you do those things right you won't have to have any intention in mind. It will just happen.

Ephesians 5:28-So ought men to love their wives as their own bodies. He that loveth his wife loveth himself.

Your wife needs for you to be the peace and the priest.

She looks for you to be her covering both spiritually and emotionally. She looks for you to love her.

She looks to you to help and to push her to prevail.

Chapter Notes

_____

_____

_____

_____

_____

_____

_____

_____

Chapter Four

Wisdom for the Husband

Inspired by Dr. Phillip Davis

Ephesians 5:25 Husbands, love your wives, even as Christ also loved the church, and gave himself for it.

Ephesians 5:25 And you husbands, show the same kind of love to your wives as Christ showed to the church, as he died for her. Living Bible (TLB)

Men I would like to share a few of my thoughts man to man on some truths that I have learned, observed and know to work in marriage and for making your marriage better as a husband.

It is imperative to make sure you are holding up your part of the agreement or terms so that your vows won't be null and void.

What terms am I speaking of?

I'm saying that you must have that Christ like love. That Unconditional Love with no strings attached. *Example:* I will love her as long as she stays submissive and does what I tell her to do. Wrong!

Ephesians 5:21 says we (men) are to submit ourselves one to another in the fear of God.

Christ laid down His life for us as a man, as the covering and the priest of the home you must lay down your life for your spouse by putting her needs before your own.

Jesus came to serve the church as an asset and not a liability. You can make your marriage better as a husband by learning how to see your wife as an asset, an advantage to adding strength to your life.

See her as Christ sees her as a helping hand to you and the kingdom.

Men trust me! I know sometimes we can feel the wife has it made because all the pressure and responsibility is the husband's and we are the ones that will have to answer to the Lord. So, I hear you saying so; tell me how she is an asset?

Find the answer by asking yourself these questions?

• Is she among the working class?

• Does she cook and takes care of the home?

• Is she mindful and doesn't over spend and she knows how to budget?

Real talk.

If you want to make your marriage better as a husband, change your mindset and attitude towards your wife.

Even if you feel she does not line up as an asset in those areas with your help, she can get there. _Be sure to check yourself._ *Are you meeting all of your wife's expectations?*
Are your expectations with the right heart and right motive?

1 Corinthians 11:3; But there is one matter that I want to remind you about; that a wife is responsible to the husband, her husband is responsible to Christ, and Christ is responsible to God.

To make your marriage better as a husband have a vision.

The vision shows the wife the direction that you both are going together in the marriage.

In Habakkuk 2:2 it says to Write the vision and make it plain upon tables, that he may run that readeth it.

Write the vision on paper, write it on the calendar or hang it on the refrigerator so that you both can see it continually. Have a vision for the finances and on how to spend and save money.

But keep in mind this vision and plan has to be something you both agree to do for it to work.

For success in this area:

1. **Show her why we need to save just don't tell her because we need to.**

2. **Communicate the direction you are trying to go and when you are trying to arrive.**

3. **Show her the plan and the purpose, what you are trying to accomplish with the finances.**

If she can understand the vision, she will run and support you.

Make it Plain, Explain and you will Prevail.

Chapter Notes

_____

_____

_____

_____

_____

_____

_____

_____

_____

Chapter Five

Keys to Making Marriage Better as a Husband Spiritually, Physically and Emotionally

Inspired by Dr. Phillip Davis

Keys are a very instrumental tool in life. They not only give you the ability to lock out any unauthorized entry, but they also give you the ability to lock in and secure.

Keys additionally grants one access and privilege to secured areas.

Using the proper key will give you access to wisdom with your wife and grant you continued access to her heart

Men let's use these keys to close the door and keep the enemy out of our marriage and open the door for love and longevity.

Let's walk through a few Keys:

Spiritual Key

Make God the center of your marriage and Seek God daily for your marriage.

Ask God to show you in your prayer time and reveal to you the spiritual needs for your marriage.

Ask, and God will show you His purpose and plan for your wife so that you will have a greater understanding where she is going, and so you won't become a hindrance to your wife.

Ask God to show you how to communicate with your wife. Sometimes as men we don't always know how to communicate very well.

We don't realize that our tone of voice can make a difference in the outcome of the situation. If it's positive, she communicates, responds and seeks to understand if it is negative she won't receive anything from us.

Physical Key

Allow her to pamper and spend some money on herself.

Realize she has a job too whether she works outside of the home or not. Working in the home can be just as strenuous and tedious as working outside of the home, they both hold value.

Set up allowances if she is a stay at home mom with the kids or a stay at home wife that manages the castle that you live in.

She needs funds, so she is not looking tore up from the floor up. After all, she is a representation of you and we men desire to be represented well.

Be sure she is well taken care of and looks good so that she can see herself as a beautiful woman and she can still light your fire.

Encourage her to dress nice, smell nice, and to get her feet and nails done. Now if that is not her desire it is alright but know what her desires are and encourage them.

Have not just a date night but a night of romance in every way. Husbands get creative.

Example: make a coupon book, romantic meal; if you can't cook a romantic meal go and pick up one and set it up.

Make preparations to enter into her Garden o love throughout the day. Put an I love you card in her purse.

Come on men! Set it up!

Don't make it like stealing apples; get in there and get out as quick as you can. Learn to savor the moment. Cuddle afterwards.

Don't roll over and just fall asleep talk to her and make her feel special for the entire evening.

Emotional Key

✓ Tell her how much you appreciate her.

✓ Learn how to be just a great listener and nothing else. Don't try to solve the problem!

✓ Help out with the kids and share the load.

✓ Do things with the kids besides family time to allow her time for herself.

✓ Encourage her to go to women seminars and conferences for her spiritual growth and have fun with friends and sisters in the faith. Find ways to budget this with the finances.

✓ Allow her to get away to go visit family members. Even if you can't go be sure she gets there.

Remember, this is bigger than you.

What you do now will be groomed into your sons on how to treat their wife and groomed into your daughters on what to look for in a husband.

Seek to paint the bigger picture just so that not only will you prevail in your marriage, but so that the picture is painted and the stage is set for your children and your children's children to have a passion for prevailing as well in their marriages.

Chapter Notes

_____

_____

_____

_____

_____

_____

_____

_____

_____

_____

When you play the right keys in marriage

a beautiful melody is made.

Dr. JDD

Chapter Six

Celebrating Your Husband

Inspired by Dr. Phillip Davis

Ladies, we pray this will give insight to focusing on your husband and celebrate him.

Your husband desires to be celebrated and to know that you are his number one fan in all that he does. Let me share with you a few keys on how to honor your husband.

Ephesians 5:33; Nevertheless let everyone of you in particular so love his wife even as himself, and the wife see that she reverence her husband.

Reverence means a feeling of deep respect, love, and esteem.

When I speak of reverence, I am talking about a love deeper than the surface I'm talking about having extreme love.

Four Keys to Celebrating your Husband

1. Accept your husband's position as the head of your household.

- Understand the decisions that he makes, is in the best interest of the home. Be supportive of his decisions.

- Allow your husband to be the spiritual leader in the home.

- Encourage him in his decision-making by giving positive feedback.

2. Show respect to your husband.

- Let your husband know that you believe in him.

- Never talk down to him or make him feel inferior; especially in front of others.

- Build your husband up. Proverbs 14:1

- Acknowledge his efforts to grow by focusing on the right things about him and not the bad.

- Allow him to be needed in your life.

Your husband needs to know that even with you being confident, independent and strong that he is still in high demand.

Never allow him to feel or have the question in the back of his mind; *"What am I needed here for*?" Let him know and assure him he is needed. He is not needy but needed.

3. Appreciate your Husband

- Tell him often what he does is important.

Let your husband know how you appreciate the things he does and how it makes you feel.

Let him know he is the man!

- Say thank you for the things he does.

- Be understanding when he's down, and be there to comfort him and build him up.

- Don't take the time he spends with you and the children for granted.

- Allow him to have time for himself.

- Allow him to rest not letting anything, or anyone disturbed him. Be protective of him during this period

4. Love your Husband

- Spend time alone with him with no distractions. No children, no phone calls, no text messages, no Facebook or anything else. Let it be all about him.

Make him your biggest investment, know that with an investment there always comes a return.

- Prepare a special time just for him.

- Cook his favorite meal from time to time without him asking.

- Allow him to share his dreams with you.

- Assure him that you're in this marriage to win. *(In it to win it)*

- Represent him at all times.

- Have passionate desires for him and give all of yourself to him.

Hebrews 13:4 a-Marriage is honorable in all, and the bed undefiled:

Have a fun time with him after all he is all yours and you are all his.

When your husband is celebrated, he truly sees himself as a man of valor. Your opinion of him really does matter and is valued more than you realize.

Ladies, you have the influence to build him up or to tear him down. Celebrate him, be his peace, his supporter and encourager and reap the results of what you sow into your man.

Chapter Notes

_____

_____

_____

_____

_____

_____

_____

_____

Praise and celebration to your spouse is like an injection of momentum. It releases life, love and endurance.

Dr. JDD

Chapter Seven

Wives Don't be Bad to the Bone

Proverbs 12:4 (NIV) A wife of noble character is her husband's crown, but a disgraceful wife is like decay in his bones.

I know you have heard the saying; bad to the bone and depending on how it is used we can see it as a good or offensive thing. You may see a pair of shoes, a dress or purse and say; "that is bad to the bone!" I have even heard this statement used as a compliment about someone in their area of ministry or area of expertise. The bad to the bone in which I am talking about is not a good thing.

I'm talking about a bone deep bad that can cause decay in your marriage.

Wives it is important that you represent your husband well in all that you do. How you carry yourself is a representation of your spouse.

The Bible tells us that a wife of noble character is her husband's crown. Noble means to be honorable, upright, decent and polite.

As a wife, your character in and out of the presence of your husband is important no matter where you are or what you are doing you should still be building his crown. ***Watch how you carry and conduct yourselves around the opposite sex.***

Be sure that you are never flouncing around or presenting yourself in a teasing fashion.

Imagine with me for a minute a plain crown that is given to you after you are married and it is said how you build your character as a wife will determine the number of jewels that will be placed on our husband's crown.

Titus 2:5 To be discreet, chaste, keepers at home, good, obedient to their own husbands, that the word of God be not blasphemed.

Imagine it was also said; that based how you submit to your husband by being a prudent wife from the Lord, Proverbs 19:14 will determine how polished and how many jewels his crown will have. Your prudence will determine the weight and quality of gold of your husband's crown. Will his crown have 10 karats, 15 karats or 24 karats gold?

Will it shine like pure gold or will it be a 10 karat overlay? Think about it. Based on where you are now as a wife how much would his crown weigh? Would it have enough rubies, sapphires, pearls, and diamonds placed on it to make you proud of yourself?

Will his jewels be sufficient so that people will see and really know how much you love and value your husband? In the bible days, women use to address their husbands with honor so much as to call them lord and some king.

Now; don't go getting huffy and say, "she tripping I am not calling him king."

That is not what I am saying, it's just an example, but now if you want to, that's up to you.

I am sure with doing so you will get some jewels yourself (smile).

If we asked your husband and told him to be completely honest about how you make him feel would your husband feel like the king of his home and in your life?

Ladies this is just a little something to cause us to ponder and evaluate our own selves as wives.

A wife is to be her husband's glory and should not be her husband's hell.

Ladies, I just want you to be encouraged and see the importance and value placed on being a wife. You are the peace of his life and of the home. You set the tone for everything.

Think about it if you got upset, off track and discombobulated; the entire house gets off track. You are the key ingredient in the home for keeping the harmony.

As a wife, to build that crown, there has to be a level of submission that cannot be disrupted by emotions or opinions of others.

The kind of submission that says; I am determined to be a good wife and continue to build my husband and myself.

Proverbs 31:10-12 NKJ Who[b] can find a virtuous[c] wife? For her worth is far above rubies.[11] The heart of her husband safely trusts her; So, he will have no lack of gain.[12] She does him good and not evil All the days of her life.

Look at this; the heart of her husband safely trusts her. I'm talking about a submission that his heart believes you. He can trust you with his dreams, his hurts and pain, his vision, his failures, and know that his heart is safe with you. He can trust you with his heart so much so that if he displays areas of weakness and imperfections, you will still love and respect him.

He can trust you with his heart that you will not break or destroy it if he cannot give you everything you desire and that you will stand by his side in times of struggle still loving and supporting him.

He can trust you that at all times you will do him good and not evil. *Can he trust his heart to be safe with you?*

Nothing saddens my heart more than to see a wife running down her husband.

I am not talking about sharing with a mentor about a situation and getting Godly counseling.

I am talking about running him down making him look bad or talking crazy to him in front of others in public and at home.

I have seen women talk down so much to their husbands, run them and run everything to where he has no say so in the home or in her life. Feeling that they need to have total and complete control of everything. Surely there can be no reward of jewels in that.

I remember many years ago before I was married I was young and did not have a car at the time.

I asked this lady for a ride home from work she said sure I don't drive my husband will pick me up, and we will take you home.

I asked her; "Are you sure that's alright with your spouse?" He may have something else to do when he picks you up so please check with him first and let me know.

She replied to me in a thunderous voice "I don't need to check with my husband;

He does whatever the H E double hockey sticks I tell him too!" (*She didn't spell it*).

I paused, looked at her and said okay. Remind you that is over 30 years ago, but the impact she made on me with that particular situation was not too good. Now, of course, I took the ride home even with all of that extra.

When we got to the car, she says, "We are taking her home!" Need I say more on that, and you best believe he drove me home without a word. I can vaguely remember the ride home other than her fussing at him in directing him in which way I was saying to go.

However, what I do remember is a man sitting behind the wheel that even in my young age I could see has been beat down and had no confidence.

I then later chimed in on her conversations, and it was evident no respect and not too much love for her husband was in place. If they started out like this in marriage, I don't know, but I just believe there had to be something between them at the beginning that drew them together. I'm not sure if something happened in the marriage that caused this to be the results of the action, but what I can say is something was there that should not have been.

Do I still remember her? Yes, I can still remember her name and how she looked at that time. What happened to them and where are they and did their marriage prevail?

I couldn't tell you. Was she saved or a believer at that time?

I can't say, but what I can say is I have seen this display in Christian women as well. I have seen them with the; I am the boss attitude and men just sitting there covered in shame.

The control, bossiness and demanding attitude are a decay that will destroy the bone structure of your marriage and eat away at your husband.

But a disgraceful wife is like decay in his bones. When his bones become decayed, they become brittle and break.

No man can stand on broken and decayed bones. Wives; please don't be bad to the bone.

This goes back to things discussed earlier in this book and in the book; Passion to Prevail Victory In Life.

Should you see any of these actions or attitudes within you; know that these are areas that you may need deliverance and healing so that you can actually seek to be sensitive and love your husband to the fullest. ***Hurting people can hurt others, but un-forgiveness will eat away at the core***.

I know some wives/women are more sensitive than others, *but:*
Being a woman is not about being the wife you desire to be or want to be, but it's about being the wife your husband needs you to be for him.

He needs you to be nourishment and to bring strength to his bones, and his bones are his heart, soul, and his spirit.

Remember the slogan "Milk does a body good"? Well my slogan is "A good wife does a husband good."

Independence

It saddens me to see women that are married but still act and live like they are single.

Standing on the phrase, I am an independent woman! Stating things like; "yes; I am married, but I don't need my husband; I do as I feel and come and go as I like; I am independent."

It's a great thing to be independent that means you are a person that can stand on your own and not always need a crutch to hold you up, but one thing about men; they love to be needed, and they love for you to depend on them.

Independence can be a real thing and a dangerous thing both at the same time if not displayed wisely.

In marriage, you must allow yourself to break free from some of those areas of individuality after all two have become one.

For example; running to the door and when your husband tries to open it for you and you respond, "I got it!"

Girl, we know you are capable, but remove your hand from the door and let it go. Let him open the door for you. It is alright!

Allow him to serve you in his own special way. Whether it be opening the door, repairing things around the house or just taking care of you when you are feeling under the weather, either way, it is alright to let him love you even in all of your strengths.

Enjoy being a woman with her man. Being soft and feminine is okay. Go ahead, try it (*smile*) you may just like it.

Proverbs 18:10-The name of the Lord is a strong tower: the righteous runneth into it, and is safe.

It is comforting in just knowing that in the name of the Lord that I am safe. In His name is a strong tower and His name are His arms, and when his arms are wrapped around me, I am covered and protected.

Just like your husband you are in his name, his name is now your name and when he runs into his name he is safe.

You are his fundamental pillar and spiritual supporter. In your arms are his comfort and protection.

Proverbs 31:10-11a
Who can find a virtuous woman? For her price is far above rubies.[11] The heart of her husband doth safely trust in her.

Wives let him find you as a virtuous woman.

Don't be Bad to the bone.

Chapter Notes

_____

_____

_____

_____

_____

_____

_____

_____

Wives, the adorning beauty of peace, joy and strength you release in marriage is priceless.

Dr. JDD

Chapter Eight

Real Talk

Your marriage is a significant investment. The most important thing that you can have is communication.

Communication is the number one key.

You may have a great love life, but if the communication is not secure and strong, the love making may not last long.

I pray this book has been and will be a tool to assist in taking your marriage to the next level and to excel into a greater love between you and your spouse.

Marriage is a beautiful covenant that is to be cherished and nurtured.

Now that you have taken the time to purchase this book use it as a tool in your marriage, marriage ministries, or give it to others to use as a tool in their marriage.

I pray that your marriage is blessed beyond measure and that you explore and experience all that the Lord has in store for you.

To receive a return, there must be an investment. Seek for the great return in your marriage.

If you put each other first, you both will always be first.

There is no room in your marriage for anger, bitterness, and un-forgiveness.

You and your spouse may have been through somethings in your marriage that could have destroyed it, but because of love, time, and family and because your wedding was built on a foundation, you both made a choice to stay and work things.

If you chose to stay, then you opted to forgive.

Forgiveness is not forgetting, but releasing; not reminding the spouse of the past.

It is releasing and not rehashing the past every chance you get. Or bringing up the past in the middle of an argument that has nothing to do with the current situation. Release it and do not consistently throw your past at one another every opportunity you get.

If you chose to stay, you opted to let it go and live life in the present not in the past.

For the spouse who caused the hurt.

You are to be patient and give the other spouse time and allow the trust to be built again.

You are forgiven by the Lord, so there is no condemnation, but there are consequences that can be the results of past actions. Once you have asked the Lord for forgiveness, there is no more condemnation, but please *be sure not to try and condemn your spouse out of your guilt.* They were the innocent bystander who had no part in your actions. Because of your actions, your wife or husband was left to feel vulnerable, and deal with the hurt, and with the why and to wrestle with what they could have done to cause or not to cause the situation to happen. Please support, love and allow them to mend. Even in forgiveness there are steps and time

For the spouse who caused the hurt you may bounce back a little quicker, but the one that was hurt may need a bit more time.

In that space of time, the spouse who caused the damage needs to do all they can to bring comfort, provide security and do all you can to show you are to be trusted again. ***There is no room for pride***.

Just knowing that your spouse chose to stay shows how much they actually love you, are committed to you and desire to spend the rest of their life with you.

As real talk; it's not wise to apply pressure on your spouse to just accept it and pretend like nothing happened.

It is not wise for you to keep reminding your spouse of what happened.

Once you have made a choice to forgive you have decided to let go and not look back. It's a process of working together to move forward.

A little bedroom talk

Communicate with your spouse.
Don't leave your spouse to try to figure out what you like and need and when they are not fulfilling in those areas you get frustrated.

Just tell them.
Yes, your spouse should know you intimately however, as time change needs and desires change also.

Don't be afraid to try new things with each other: As long as you both are in agreement.

Strive to keep the fire flaming in your marriage.

Remember:
   Marriage is honourable in all, and the bed undefiled: but whoremongers and adulterers God will judge. Hebrews 13:4

It's all a matter of having the Passion To Prevail

CONCLUSION

I pray this book has been and will be a tool to assist in taking your marriage to the next level and to excel your heart into a greater love between you and your spouse.

Marriage is a beautiful covenant that is to be cherished and nurtured.

Now that you have taken the time to purchase this book use it as a tool in your marriage ministries, to give to others and to use as a continual tool and reference in your personal marriage.

I pray that your marriage is blessed beyond measure and that you explore and experience all that the Lord has in store for you and your marriage.

In order to receive a return there has to be an investment. Seek for the great return in your marriage. *If you put each other first you both will always be first.*

It's a matter of having the passion to prevail!

ABOUT THE AUTHOR
AND HER HUSBAND

Dr. Jeanette D. Davis is the author of Passion To Prevail: In Marriage and Passion To Prevail: Victory in Life from the Passion to Prevail Series.

Jeanette has been married to the love of her life Phillip for 28 years. They have two adult children Shanae and Jamar and a grandson Elijah. Both are Licensed Ordained Elders with a Doctorate Degree in Biblical Studies and a Master of Arts and a Master of Divinity from Minnesota Graduate School of Theology. Jeanette is also a graduate from Eagles International Authors Institute. **Phillip and Jeanette are a Dynamic Duo** husband and wife team that not only share the same name but by the grace, love and thankfulness to God for their marriage gaining strength, wisdom and knowledge to succeed over obstacles and challenges, they share the same spirit and heartbeat in helping others build healthy relationships and succeed in their marriages. They have been ministering to marriages for over 15 years teaching at various couple events, marriage seminars, conferences and retreats. It is Phillip and Jeanette's heart's desire that couples are not just married but enjoy the covenant that they share in marriage. It is their passion that couples thrive to reach levels of love that conquers all.

Their ministry and heart's desire is to strengthen, push and encourage couples to stand and stay true to their vows by having a *PASSION TO PREVAIL IN MARRIAGE.*

Contact Dr. P&J Davis at

ptpvictory@gmail.com

www.passiontoprevail.com

www.ingramcontent.com/pod-product-compliance
Lightning Source LLC
LaVergne TN
LVHW022323080426
835508LV00041B/2390